OX-EYE

Anne Rouse lives in East Sussex. Her fifth collection, *Ox-Eye*, was published by Bloodaxe in 2022, appearing 14 years after her previous book, her retrospective *The Upshot: New and Selected Poems*, which included the new poems of *The Divided* (2008), along with selections from her first three critically acclaimed earlier collections, *Sunset Grill* (1993) and *Timing* (1997) – both Poetry Book Society Recommendations – and *The School of Night* (2004). *The Upshot* was a *Times Literary Supplement* Book of the Year in 2008. A former health worker, she has been a Hawthornden Fellow, and a Royal Literary Fund Fellow at the University of Glasgow (2000-02), Queen's University, Belfast (2004-05), and the Courtauld Institute, London (2008). Her short plays have been given rehearsed readings in Edinburgh and Hastings in the UK and in Virginia in the US. You can find her on Twitter @rouseanne

ANNE ROUSE

Ox-Eye

BLOODAXE BOOKS

ISBN: 978 1 78037 608 0

First published 2022 by
Bloodaxe Books Ltd,
Eastburn,
South Park,
Hexham,
Northumberland NE46 1BS.

www.bloodaxebooks.com
For further information about Bloodaxe titles
please visit our website and join our mailing list
or write to the above address for a catalogue.

Supported using public funding by
**ARTS COUNCIL
ENGLAND**

For John Walker

Cover design: Neil Astley & Pamela Robertson-Pearce.

Printed in Great Britain by Bell & Bain Limited, Glasgow, Scotland, on
acid-free paper sourced from mills with FSC chain of custody certification.

CONTENTS

Polaroid

Two novelists, a poet, *c*. 1960.
Posterity is taking the photograph.
They wear thin, black ties;
luck prowls behind each grin.
Posterity has already taken to them.

In front of the tall one is a woman,
her eyes screwed up against the hard, noon light.
Her dress is white like a carnation,
or sea foam, against their buoyant gazes.
Their dark suits are like a wood,

and she, reluctant, half-ducking the camera's eye,
(which would ignore her if it could),
an errant vine. Her work is hidden:
the starlit ramble round the country garden,
the making liveable of inching lives.

Theirs is the public exhalation; hers, the in-breath.

Moonrise 2021

Moonrise is unfamiliar,
arc of fire in a wash of blue,
plucked from night's sleeve,
blotched disc of sun-glow.

Waddya want, a medal?
My late, wisecracking pre-war father.
Whatever's hanging there,
brass or gilt, yes I do.

Freckled looking-glass, reflective
of our pocked aureole,
a stain has spread in its hollows.
Someone at prayer. A curving embryo.

Landfill

It wasn't on the map, that spot we found.
Dogs ran, whirling at their owners' shouts,
on the scrubby recreation ground;
we skirted a wood of hopeful oaks, and crossed
a second copse to a green: a hidden field
revealing, soon enough (a manhole cover, rusted vents)
that its lustrous grass, its collared doves, its tangled
fringe of buddleia and Queen Anne's Lace,
rested on ravioli tins and Rich Tea packets,
the hairline-cracked, the chucked-in-rage, the town's
miasmic secrets, but mostly just
on the indifferent residue of days – and walked it round
as if its buried future were still ours.

Feeny's Yard

A bantam cock, a party boy, dressed up,
trails fitfully after the big hens,
his tail-feathers a Revelations sun
in the last light.

The hens dawdle into Feeny's yard,
and one, with a stagger and dip, succumbs
to the waiting Moby of a rooster.
The Leghorn crows, the bantam draggles after.

The hens drift on, becoming dusk
– and how familiar it is,
that small bonfire in the mud,
amongst the dubious and unseeing.

Finish Line

(from Ian Berry's photograph, 'The Royal Ascot, England 1975')

It's Royal Ascot, moments before the start.
A dove-suited bon vivant strides from the lens,
while a porter rattles towards us, pushing crates.

The flâneur's buoyant, fixed on Rapallo in the second,
Pimms, the tote; the hireling trundles worriedly
behind his quota. (The boxes must be stacked outside the tent.)

A summary Queen of the Rites, a faery arbiter
of this back-to-back encounter in the field,
would order Hat to genuflect, and smartly; Toiler to be fed.

I'm dreaming. For both it's late.
It would tax the art of tutor or masseuse
to soothe the anxious labourer from the part.

In sleep, the jagged hands still move.
I wish him a pensioned corner in the nearest snuggery,
soon, and rebellious children. It's in the bone.

Seyton

The queen, my Lord, is dead.

It's the washing.
Mrs Seyton on her knees all night:
blood, wax, stink of their fears.
('Cold-blooded' – right!)
He wants his armour on; his armour off;
sends me out; calls me back.
Seyton doesn't need to eat or sleep.
I said, didn't I, we're in for it now,
they've bottled. (Why did he think
the women were crying? Onions?
His eyes were like pie-tins.)
But whatever he goes and does,
in the end, it's always, call Seyton.
'Where's Seyton?' he says.
'I could crown him.'

Night of the Monkey Puzzle Tree

Green ziggurat, it jigsaws the view
with needle-tipped, serrated boughs,
lizard teeth in outsized jaws,
haunting the suburban present,
a country beyond accident.

The monkeys triumph, currently.
The Holocene age evolved between
its scissor branches: book and screen,
traffic growling up the ridge,
began under a blackthorn hedge.

Dwindling to whitened clemency,
the slow night ends; its brawlers pale;
each flash of claw has left our sentinel
unmarked and unimpressed; only loftier,
rooted in gore, attempting the hereafter.

Across its jagged workman's weave
outriders of the sun prevail
and now the uneven shadows steal
into the morning's reckoning
through every baffled dream.

The Town

You arrive at a ruined barn
pocked and flecked with lichen;
dried stalks of hemlock levelling like spears.
This is the town when it first eyes you.

A couple of pre-war shops, wares assorted.
Frantic in the sea breeze, a banner for a fête;
trays of novelettes whitening with rain.
The town that will turn a penny, if it must.

Then there's the town that pleases itself
between yellow cliffs, stucco and ragstone.
Whether passing through or asleep in a doorway,
on trickling afternoons you vanish, quite.

But this town fades too, in its salt mist,
part of an endlessness that comes and goes,
glimpsed through the aspens:
a silvered blue, half-indistinct from sky.

To the Night Market

I've been on this road or one like it.
In the dark it's a grey outline,
potholed macadam underfoot
curving on to the vanished town.

On the way to the night market,
the thin laughter rises
like the wisps from cigarettes
when I ask, what place is this?

I wander between square and station,
between station and square,
until a voice saying, *yes, love*
reveals them, the original pair,

in close-knit cap and cock-eyed trilby,
sitting on a step, and I lead them away
to lit warrens where the glad buffet
awaits on long tables, and shades retreat

that we might stay, and eat.

Ballad of the She

Under the blade of the sun,
I heard a confession:
a daimon had said to a she,
'Come lie with me,
be only mine,' and, frayed
into longing, she obeyed.

Now, maiden, fly,
take up your sack of joy.
The merry rivers run,
the tired thief is gone.
Fling off, as you find shelter,
faces you used to wear:

damsel, sleeper, silent one,
odalisque and mannequin.
Live out your truest word.
This was what I heard
(which was said, and done)
under the blade of the sun.

Haymaking

The bales had been stacked by late-working farm hands
By nightfall, in the peace,
after which they hared off in the lorry,
as the sun begins to well up,
with a stack the size of a chalet, under a spinning amber light.
purple extends over the hedgerows
The bales left behind lay here and there
and coolness drifts in from the copse.
in lines, long barrows, on the under-grass,
The sun crinkles behind a fir, and liquefies.
conveying the oat, dry smell of the hay.

I knew from of old the rasp of hay,
In the country house hotel,
the weight of a bale, twine cutting the palms.
we're only what is,
Over and again the tarpaulin-shaded trailer rattles off –
– there being no snags
behind cab and driver, under the late sky.
catching at us from the big before...
A crane arm lifts the bales.

Late Swim

In earnest now, braced for grim waftings
from the North Sea, I run down one evening
to try. A scraping tide; low-level clouds;
sandbars. An Indian summer sifts the chill.
Its fading hazes the rivulets and sheen.

Stripped, I'm in, affronted, as long caverns
spill late reds; turn, and idle on the swells,
while brief shapes cross a twilit promenade.
Indifference and night lend me the place;
allow the green-grey shot with silver-white

to release me, in weighted footfalls back
through a waning sweep; running gear resisting
the wet skin. And ascend suddenly to dark
– gain the ridge of the public gardens, and look down
on lily pads against a green-black pond.

Greetings from Hastings Pier

The pier's in ashes; we're off the news at six.
Struts and seaward reach are bare as staves.
Belgian schoolgirls sketch the raw pilings in charcoal.
Gloved workers rake the debris off the beach.

The pier grows cold, a wet crow on a ledge.
Tankers file in a progress from the veins
of the estuary: the village warriors sleep;
the ruined keep superbly faces France.

(The cliff tops belong to neither, only May.)
The weather kiosk's crescent moon is fixed with rust.
A graph insists the Channel's warmer than it was,
that 1943 saw far less sun than any other year.

Offshore breezes. Outlook fair. A trio in shorts
– fleshy, tattooed, gleeful – run down to the misty sea.

Change

Whether you take the next boat to Taipei
or crouch in the rippling barleycorn,
she'll find you anyway.

Fly to the nearest meteor
– she'll blow your houses in.
She'll know just where you are.

Shun her, she'll creep in underfoot like rootlings.
Thwart her, she'll bide her silky time.
Betray her, she'll bring you down, flapping grey wings.

Moments you'll have before her gusts and rain.
Make your three wishes.
Meet her eye, and run with her again.

Request to a Neighbour

You knock, she waves you in
for a swirl of quiet gossip
over Hobnobs and Ceylon.

Enter the son and husband
she caters to with such finesse.
Next door, hi, you venture,

minding how you go.
Any one of them might parley, singly.
Together they're of one blood.

Diagonal across the gate, the father
coughs too much; the son's long-averted jade-
brown eyes are closing, set in shade.

All power to her, cleaning in Marigold gloves
what love fashions. You can see the joins.

The Builder's Mates

I've heard the builder's mates
talking about their father.
They say, 'Shift it to the right
about a half a centimetre...
you've still got a hairline gap
along the architrave...' They say,
'...and that's why we've cut
ourselves off from him'
– tenderly, squaring up hour by hour
against unremitting matter:
drill-bits, cinder blocks,
barrow-loads of paling mortar,
as it grows under their hands,
the unyielding town.

Inconsequence

Drowsing on the steel fire steps
that end in ferns and wallflowers,
you hear a rasping. In come the bag men.
The evening, a cinder, drops into their bag.
Workaday words are said.
The clouds are water vapour.
A flash of wings means prey.
A sail, lit up for a time, is heading in,
under tremendous shadows.
It will disappear. But I've seen.

Fling

Hello, darling. I was proud of that.
(A year had passed,
the visitation felt abrupt.)
A hose stream eddied down
Ashburnham Hill;
ran coldly on, relentlessly ad hoc.
The families toiled up from
the church school.
I heard your answering voice
above a lorry's sliding bass,
its gruffest note, sustained.
What oscillates, is us.

Cyclops in Cythera

We've freed ourselves. Neither of us sleeps alone.
Three winters on, this squalling is just weather.
Doves, grey deacons, haver in the eaves.
Torn clouds resume their westering.

Out of the cave that led from you, dear Terror,
I ran seaward as the boulders fell, yards off,
rattling like coins. Your bellowing grew tinny, small;
a dry leaf eddying, the rock-face sealed behind.

I pretended, of course, that you peered after me,
a tower darkening around an eye,
trembling in a haze that ebbed and stained,
Pharos, a lamp for inbound craft to sail by

– until the horizon blinked, and overturned.
Now the trees may swarm; gusts chivvy the bells,
as if our charts or instruments were down;
as if your one-eyed image bleeds, and hovers

– but it's a rose window, this, welling with day,
as every airless chamber overruns.
I lift the latch, lean out and drink the sun:
an absence, a carolling of bells.

The Waves, and a Bang

Topaz vistas curling in
turn monotone as drunk clouds stray,
until their pewter sheens like platinum.

They fall onto the beach, in lacy hoopla.
Their tricklings drain around the jetsam.
They pass, these waves, into the galaxies,

Harping on that original event,
boomtown, moment zero: black
diamond death's burst seed, with life in it.

It Greens Again

It greens again, as if dressing for a fête.
Glad rags wave, hucksters warble in the copse.
The show's the thing: forget the seedy runners
underground, the last year's rot and weight,

the dance duplicitous: this evening we decide,
as winged replicas bid fretfully to hatch,
and blowsy come-ons veil the angling spores,
like chaste observers that we'll sit outside

– although the glade exhales our oxygen
and we're bound to the self-same waltz
(obdurate ephemera, insisting that clods
transmogrify, according to a cloud-capped vision) –

clocking our native triumph from afar: a headlong
rush into jouissance, tallying abundance
in a cistern of rain, a bush, a bee-hung spire;
twinned at the crooked root: torch singer, and song.

Uncertain Ode

This is safe water, the bedroom striped
in twilight, behemoth & armies moving
elsewhere. White words of the moon.

They're emptying the flat next door.
All her things are going: silver brushes,
ormulu, porcelain terrier, throaty hullo.

Reviewing the day's accidents:
a blaze on the railings, amassed clouds.
The light works free, is barred again

by – apparent – immensities.
(You're not untouched, it concerns you,
you will be wanted.)

A Thank You Note

The past welled up. I recognised the place.
Willows, inn tables. It all came back:
striated woods, the drizzled sheen
on the canal, a rustling toad,
smell of drenched clay, and how alone I was.

But this was new: how one good evening
earthed the spot – our trio's jaunt across
the water meadows; the wavering
last light under the bridge
– as fitting as a name put to a face.

The Morvoren

Maid of the sea (Cornish)

Miles inland, against the gloom
of a country chapel, I discover her effigy
diving in reverse, arms uplifted
to the constellations.

She catches me up, protesting,
to the reefs of bone, where the fishes loom
sudden, and blackening.
She dandles and croons, she echoes.

It's the seabed certainly, but it's not the end.
End, end, ripe orisons to the nervy shoals.
Her trinket, her bibelot, she'll lull me to rest
on the samphire road.

Morvoren (Variation)

Cast about in the moonlit chapel:
the morvoren, surfacing, swims free,
her dark curves wet from gannet dives.

Forgive the wooden stare, the crudity.
A later hand has carved her oak gifts
into mirror and ship, despoiling

face, fruit, comb –
but this demoiselle of the glittering fishtail
is unabashed, and surges home

as green waves swell,
tracing out the sea kale on a cowrie shell
with unseen fingers of alabaster, and pearl.

Ode to a Puritan

(The ancient carving of a mermaid in a church
in Zennor, Cornwall, was defaced centuries ago.)

Zennor's mermaid dandles a toy galleon
and a quince. The visitor carves a comb
and looking-glass; chisels out her face.
In the chapel's twilight, he re-names her 'Vanity'.

(But spares the fishtail, that embellishment,
Greek merchants scaring rivals off the trade routes.)
As a god she'd walked the East, soothing
the childless, weighing a caul in her red hands.

To burn the idols is one thing. Annulling their gifts
lit up the machinery of your own ascent:
the soul's strict audit; grizzled self-communing;
time kept on a chain.

You came emptied from the martyr's block
into the wealth of kings.
The women and the workmen stood,
awaiting your wrecked pleasure.

The sermon ends. You range, unwaking,
stamping on Belial and razing Jericho,
offering up a pocket-knife to the Lord of broken things
– and she plunges into the undergrove

of all your reckonings, your night thoughts
in the cradling of the waves.

From the Dark Tower Came

Picturing one night your former life,
I walk to your old house, myself a child.
Your wiry mother's just inside the threshold,
punishing the Draloned stairway with a broom.
Her cast-off beige gloves detain a matching handbag.
You're reading comics in your room.

'Benny', the new Bendix, jostles and soaps your smalls.
A cat lies low, banished from chair or bed, under
its rolling eye. All that's needed happens, or is going to:
you'll leave, look about you, and get married.
Her Mini will breeze through the town square
for Battenberg with company wives, quicksilver errands

... and now her husband's home from work,
your superheroes save New York.

Man Ironing

Sunday night. You pick up an iron in a cold room.
It hisses, and long Lethe vapours roll
over Monday's wraith, that long welter of creases.

Next morning though, the white shirt preens,
relieved of angles, endowed with you,
hurrying off to the manager's chat, the phone's peremptory.

Almost, you could be anyone, until you climb
the muffled stairs: strip down to the bleached
t-shirts of your youth. We embrace, and return.

Monterey

Hard-up once, between rented flats, I went for a room at King's Cross.
It was late to be looking on a July night.
I walked along a road of B&Bs, off-key translations of travel:
Shangrila, Imperial, The Heights. A couple turned on glimpsed stairs.
Curtains floated over a screen's blue light.

It was hot, too; peopled, NO VACANCY all down the terraced line.
A man sat slumped in a doorway. 'You can stay…here,'
– a camp bed, for 19 pounds. His face sagged over a t-shirt logo'd,
Monterey. He said that he'd been a police sergeant in Algiers.
The reception ticked, footsteps kept time in the twilit square.

I pulled off my trainers in this anteroom. He came in though.
'Sorry but I need to sleep here for a moment'; lay down, his thick
back to me as I stood, tensed. 'Please put your arms around.'
I held him, thinking of backroom cells, of singeing jolts, of flex,
a good half-hour until he started, went. I slept the night, and left at six.

The Scholars' Hostel

For the convenience of its guests, the Scholars' Hostel
provides iron toilet cubicles, painted a pale mustard; chain pulls
with wooden handles; brass bolts, exposed pipes, an asylum's group bath.
On the spacious landing, a wax Madonna clasps two lilies.
Missing a drawer, handles, patches of finish, a mahogany cupboard lours
over a red carpet frayed to a dishcloth. Go further in: enquire.

Were there dusty sweets, a grandfather clock, a freckled mirror at reception?
Were the scholars, that evening, mute as grey swans, as one by one we
tripped downstairs to dine, wearing our severe, or bewildered expressions
Did I imagine the man with lamentable breath, an out-of-work editor –
the be-cardiganed crowd in the TV lounge, frankly defeated;
the blotched counterpane, the smirched tiles, the chipped walls,

as if we'd been pulled, unresistingly, through a maelstrom,
and left our panicky marks and prints, the night going down with all hands?

Before I Left on Friday

Just before the dawn crept up,
with the light still on as if sleep had ambushed me,
I woke up to the room's reproach.
A buzz, or a sob, had been interrupted.
A fly crawled overhead, but the walls
had nothing to give it – nor did the formal curtains,
nor the painting of a lake.
It circled, recalling leafier air,
until its droning dreamed in me.
I got up to push a door open into blackness,
and flailed it out, into the familiar new.

High Wall

Behind wall and tree you could hear an alley
where lorries backed in, to the kvetching of a drill.
Ivy grew over the wall, and I set out marigolds,
little suns against the grime, and forgot to replace them when they died.

Nothing ever went wrong. The windows stuck shut,
the crab tree toppled. The bricks stood worn, and high
– until I climbed out, into nothing's weeds and blight,
and felt what was hidden: a tearing anger at the living

– a gash in the earth, and turned up the ground
to bring on the dry, flecked seeds of grass
– the green of which had arrived in the loam
this morning, when I crouched and looked with you and the child.

Graffiti

A first name – scratched with a bent nail
on the storm fence by the boarded-up hospital,

at the edge of a disused car park where we cycle,
round and round, above the Channel with its sail

– for you is one-syllable, bold like your hand, as under a marquee
of cloud you squat by a fence running over a cliff, and carefully

incise the block letters on the weathered rail,
and I turn the blind eye, riding around our circle.

Your father's the stars and the sun – but, kneeling,
you call to me; next to your name you write mine.

Heel

Roaming Sedlescombe fields,
near Battle – no lark or corncrake
hereabouts in thirty years – the heel dips,
betrayed: a subaltern, badly booted.

Thetis with the hair like wheat, grasps
her newborn's foot; dangles him headlong,
blue, dipped into deathless Styx.
He'll leave his sandalled crescent arc

on foreign sands. Diva, fate's coming for you.
A tenpence blister scrapes right off,
a raw heart in the heel, palpitating to the chug
of the haymaker backcombing the field:

stubble, heel traps,
under its hefty black-ridged tyres,
its scrambling blade-edge,
the grasses overthrown.

Again

Blueish dusk pools in the public gardens.
I pull the curtains to against the street
and balustrade, white chessmen in a row.
The room's chastened, unlit.

Out back, parallel old-brick walls,
adjacent gardens – shrubby fastnesses
where Eve might sit, under a pergola
– exhale an even quiet.

The sun glints out. Moving from window
to window, I enlist the lamp.
There is no health in us, I'd hear, a child
in choir robe and cassock (vermilion, as sin),

and still each nightward turn's illuminated,
and twilight's brought to lulling dark,
a fairytale grandmother. Who to thank?
Or simply hold each other.

Notes from a Moon Station

Reliquary of streets and flowers
swinging its dust around an elder star.
Engines left behind for the divers.
Topaz earthlight. At lunar midnight,
I fall into the ecstatic false sublime.

These apparitions float to us:
a threshold, tiled cream and russet.
Speckled flagstones.
They were blacking the lane by the gate.
That wrinkled skein. Acheron.

Mt Tambora glowed in our year of winter.
We circled the factory cities and the hungry plains:
the fires, racked walls, inundations.
From the first, we wanted to live.

Even now, the four messengers hover.
They deliver nightly to the camps: wormwood, laurels, prophecy.
Their garments bell out, they're motionless.
We're done, though, done with their four
swords meeting at star point, overhead.

Lead on, I shout, but they do not move.

Oil

I

The oil wells up through a valley of bone, floods from every
vat and line:

naptha, phosphates, plastic swill adrift in the Pacific doldrums,
motor oil, acetone, ethanol, jet fuel, gasoline, kerosene, ancient
Kowloon flame-pits drying salt, rain-slicked walls of Babylon,
tarry graves of mastodon and elk.

The ocean gives up its dark load.

II

In an arc-lit glare, a white ship's crew
is burning off thin tranches of the spill.

A clutch of sea crabs teem in a babble of smoke,
their turbulence signalling for miles.

III

Mute in the under groves
with the first attendants

mercury arsenic water salt
a black slur pulsing

over the sands
to the mansion of the rocks

relinquishing its upstart powers
to the sun and wind

a fifth element, descending
through the cells and corridors

to the circumnavigating mind,
unfurled in wordless sleep

the oil gutters from the emphatic city
turbines macadam airstrips tarshacks

in worlds made, broken and made again.

Speech Act

Words were for
the emissaries on earth,
not us: earth

– unheard and treacherous,
complicit; coerced.
Men took oath by *Him*;

our vows, soft, to them.
Out of the hell of Eden,

I walk, I swear.

Ildeth at Bela

(Ildeth: in Hebrew tradition, Lot's wife)

Gomorrah's gone, we're all taking it in.
The spring's in eclipse. Branches claw, gale-struck;
fields merge, white negatives, and resist the eye.
Orchards and sheep pens drowse on its brink.

Sodom's hidden and still, a gully of ash.
Breathless on a high slope, eluding
a wildcat flame, Lot hears her lost cry.
Tell it in Zoar: her slender obelisk over-tops the plain.

Look for the maiden, unbound and fled
from inelegant slave routines. Her salt-white stone
thrills with first light where the winds reach Bela,
as if the siege has ended, and yields to day.

Warriors

(Belfast)

They drive hell-bent as smoked-out bees;
slouch, backs to the wall, in The Rock or Lena's;
make their U-turns tight like Vs.
Rip stories out of pin-drop silence.
If a man pixelates in light, these nights,
it's a Catherine wheel; a PR blitz, a migraine. .
They snatch at chances – cocaine, robbery, vice –
like matrons overturning jumble.
They survive the peace.

A Calenture

calenture: a form of delirium formerly supposed to afflict
sailors in the tropics, in which the sea is mistaken for green
fields. [OED]

This sun is pitiless. Its face against ours,
scourger, greenish gong – by evening a carbuncle
on the steaming isles. Blackness drops utterly.
Scrimshaw, a bone flute: a handful of north
in a swag-bag traverses my equator. I'm naked,
heat-bathed, strung in my hammock, wrapped
spider's prey. I hope that this finds you well.

The nubs of ivy bud late under old leaf fall.
A green tunnel swallows the slip of a path.
Gather me valerian. A frog trills, cornered,
splodged clump, slack throat pulsed
and up – a collared dove, to the hills.
I lie on tuffets, sheep-mucked. Go lark, then,
before the clouds fissure, and rail.

A Lothario

He's still eye-deep in Eros – jackdaw walk
and broody hymns, adrenal frazzle:
that shivery richesse, that joyboy dazzle;
the tricks, the turns, the trysts and pillow talk;
the cracked entreaties, vigils by the phone;
the late manoeuvres, witty like a play;
observances on Valentinus' Day –
still swims in living waters, quite alone.

Obits

Vi rejected the modern world with all its ills.
So Vi's a homespun sage among the jonquils
– no more the doyenne, over roll-ups
and the *Express*, of The Jar at Leytonstone.

Vi's flat: a camp-bed, folding chair,
pooling sink clotted with rust and hair,
a floor inlaid with newsprint, gauzy tufts
off a burst eiderdown.

After an awkward loss, who'd carp at how
the littleness falls away:
X built a school; Y pulled a friend to safety.
Vi winks, and waves a glass at me.

Domestic Animal

Despite lapses from grace,
wailing in the alley; a resorting, if coaxed,
to a pounce on a frizzle of string,
there's a dignity, unspent.

A watching, primed with blood.
They escape, with lithe carelessness,
the hurly-burly; leave us to
the carousel of striving.

Report on Local Damage

The walnut tree shakes
its assent – a tossed
marionette in a billow
of leaves between
telephone wires, its
dervishing watched
by the staid terraced houses
– to the lifting storm.

It dangles a solitary wire,
black lightning
against the bindweed,
or a cat's toy.
Flailing, it attests
to its own emerging,
its long exhale of oxygen;
its night cry, too, falling
and subsiding.

Clematis

How it's a flame of snow.
How it breaks open, in the ceiling, a skylight.
How silences conspire to join at its tipped bud.
How it outshines all but eyes.

How it jolts the air with becoming.
How it predicts grace at the last.
How it aims its tiny roar at our placidity.
How it accompanies our reading as if it were the only song.

Found Poem for Beryl Markham

No map I have flown by has ever been lost
or thrown away. I have a trunk containing continents.
This map: the ragged coastline on your skull?
After twenty-one record trans-Atlantic hours,
I crashed at Cape Breton in a Vega Gull.
These faint trails? The claws and teeth of a lion.
This slight, cranial valley? *A stallion threw me.*
This pale road? *A sword-cut from a Nandi boy*
I'd beaten at wrestling. You've been prodigal enough,
spent each hour and named your loves.
Tell the nurse and the ancient admirers, the rest
is hidden like the Sudd. 'An interminable slough...
men cannot walk in it.' There is no map of the interior.

Louse

So this is where you lie low, after ascending
with a fortune of legs, the serried Pyrenees:
scuttling into view, blithe iota, chancer.

Goldilocks disdains you, and I've called you out,
threshing and threshing with a fine machine,
until the old trails end, and all about you is clean

porcelain – then do you drop, minute particular?
Or cling, upended, to a redundant hair
in a light foam of shampoo

– clutching at gleaming straws again,
below you the deluge.

Suburban Pastoral

Behind the waking houses,
spiders' webs and ivy, flecked
with sawdust from the Council's hired blades.
Willowherb, ragweed, sea poppy.

A Victorian fantasia. Mansion of flats.
Down the cliff stair a baffled spring
meanders through the detritus
of street drinkers. Coconut palm, in fruit.

Out to the Channel, and a bench
rutted with initials. Sun-warmed,
desultory, they watch singly, in pairs,
as silhouettes ply oars like filaments.

A tanker passes, the surf replies;
exceeds itself until in them,
that pair, its syncopation (the almost
infinite) is indeed, infinite.

The Beat

(i.m. Irene Rouse)

The train slows in my native city
though a tunnel studded with arc lights.
The new arrives like it arrived before:
scrape-skinned, flooding, shining,
with a wail, into a stranger's grip.

In her *Conch Shell*, white, beige and aqua,
the surf rolls into the room.
Peacefully, at home. The tunnel gives way
to a rusted chain-link fence.
The beat goes thready, stops.

At Chincoteague

At Chincoteague, the canoe
slides through blue-black and its reflection

until the bay smooths to a lake
and still us, almost motionless,

peering into the altered dark
for the canal's mouth: the way home.

It's then, as the paddles revive their sweep,
that we strike phosphorescent green and blue

– the jellyfish, a ghostly blooming
and subsiding yards from shore:

lighting for the drift, and the letting go.

Return to Sender

It's a no man's land: rusted side-gate,
gully of last year's leaves and briars,
grey aureoles of dandelion – sentinels
against the neighbours' stucco and rose.

I wait for the greetings to wash over me.
A moth beats, flimsy, against the entry light.
Brown water rots in the terrace's troughs and urns.
I can smell its marshy stagnancy.

Then I'm like the prodigal's brother, railing
at the vines, *why's that master death so welcome here?*
I go to the feast, eventually, and wonder
at the conjurors, their daylight getaway.

They sweep out, their sequinned trains trailing
in the rutted driveway, to the wooded road
– as love, like a stooping bodyguard,
walks with them to the end.

The Maying

I rode south to the saltwater town,
and the ramshackle porch
blindly flowering with May.

In the warm evening, we strolled
to the peeling movie house.
It was Okinawa, and the fighting in caves.

I watched: neither of them blinked
at the pierced omphalos.
At their fierce, old loss.

Mayday.
Mayday.
The bayonet haunts me.

High waters on the causeway
tossed by the wind: to one side, scintilla;
whitened foam on the other.

Two dead drakes, throats of iridescent green.
A shrill voice, *piccolo*, 'She ran right over it.
It was fluttering its wings.'

Strawberries & blueberries of the underworld.
At the counter in the ice cream shack,
a radio report of an exploding star:

Supernova, with a tail like a running
peacock or a fox, a threaded awl arriving
at the pinprick, *now*, hauling its future light.

Tying a scarf where the iris flourished,
taffeta lifting to the balmy spring:
'banners & pennants!' she called – when word came

that a friend had shot himself in the night.
'Yes, it was *de trop*, and this is what we went through.'
Green shoots of the canna lily;

the pink freedoms of the azalea,
and the wound in the omphalos:
rings of barbed wire, becoming the rose.

Grotto

An outsized conch-shell blown
by wealth, by history's men,

it glistens with its light cargo
washed up from planetary distances

– abalone, flute and fan, king crab –
to the city wharves, and set in mortar

on this great estate by local girls
who were nameless even then,

and whose mosaic lines converge,
unbroken mother-of-pearl,

a giver's cup, forever running over.

ACKNOWLEDGEMENTS

Some of these poems have appeared in *Acropolis Journal, Acumen, Bad Lilies, Cardiff Review, Degenerate Art, Edinburgh Review, Feral* (USA), *Magma, New Linear Perspectives*, PoetryFilm website, *Poetry Review, Poetry Salzburg Review, Poetry Wales, Punk Noir* and *The Times Literary Supplement*. 'Oil' grew out of a collaboration with the artist Emily Johns, as part of her touring exhibition from 2010 onwards, 'Conscious Oil'. It appears in the pamphlet *Conscious Oil: Myth and Mind in the Age of Petroleum* (2010) by Emily Johns, Milan Rai and Anne Rouse. 'High Wall' featured in *The Best British Poetry 2012*, edited by Sasha Dugdale and Roddy Lumsden (Salt Publishing, 2012). 'Request to a Neighbour' appeared in *The Brown Envelope Book*, an anthology on austerity and disability, edited by Kate Jay-R and Alan Morrison (Culture Matters, 2021). 'Fling' has featured in an online video commissioned by the Jermyn Street Theatre, London, read by the actor Burt Caesar. Thanks are also due to Cristina Silva of Time etc for invaluable practical advice.

Finally, my partner, John Walker, has been an unfailing source of encouragement and perceptive comment.